The Turn of the Tiller,
The Spill of the Wind

The Turn of the Tiller, The Spill of the Wind

Poems by

Nancy Austin

Kelsay Books

Copyright 2019 Nancy Austin. All rights reserved.
This material may not be reproduced in any form, published,
reprinted, recorded, performed, broadcast,
rewritten or redistributed without the explicit
permission of Nancy Austin.
All such actions are strictly prohibited by law.

Cover design: Shay Culligan

ISBN: 978-1-949229-97-4

Kelsay Books Inc.

kelsaybooks.com
502 S 1040 E
A119
American Fork, Utah
84003

To sisters Linda and Sue, and all my family members, including Gary, a benevolent recipient of many paper airplane poems; to my Northwoods writing group, The PaperBirch Poets (once again and always, I am grateful, grateful), and to the look on my poetry-apostate husband's face when I make him listen to a new poem:

The Breakthrough

My husband, who has no use for poetry
responded *Wow!* with a chortle of appreciation
as I made him listen to my latest poem.

Overtaken by the joy of this connection
(he usually shrugs and walks away)
I asked him, Wow? What does that mean?

That means, he said from the other room,
a big, hairy spider just marched out
of the woodpile I carried in.

Acknowledgments

A kind thank you to the editors of the following journals for publishing these or earlier versions of the following poems:

Ariel Anthology: "To Her Daughter at the Onset"

Bramble: "After the Shootings, a Congregation"; "Funeral Flowers"

From Everywhere a Little: A Migration Anthology: "Opportunity"

Portage Magazine: "Where I Dwell" "Return to the Ice Caves" "Songbird, Raptor"

Gyroscope Review: "Let Ornithology Call the Day"

The Artist's Muse: An Exhibit: "En Plein Air" "Drifters"

The Wisconsin Poets Calendar, 2019: "Bowls of July"

Contents

The Aerodynamics of the Muse	13
The Secrets of Trees	14
Songbird-Raptor	15
Drifters	16
The Last Time	17
My Grown Daughter Asks About Her Grandma	18
Funeral Flowers	19
Bowls of July	20
The Breakup	21
To Her Daughter, at the Onset	22
Tributaries of a Dream	23
The Last of the Lightbulbs	24
In Autumn We Purchase Northwoods Lakefront Property	25
The Sun's Position	26
After the Shootings, a Congregation	27
Opportunity	28
Fifth Floor Children's Hospital, Providence, RI	29
Little Girl Dancing in a Short Museum Film	30
Plough Horses and Carriages	31
Le Jardin de Claude Monet	32
The Return to the Ice Caves	33
Incoming	34
How the Universe Guides Us	35
My Morning Buzz	36
Toads on the Lake Road	37
Let Ornithology Call the Day	38
The Reset	39
Flashbacks of a Retiree: Call Me Ginny	40
Endangered	42
A Heart Swells	44
The Last Flicker	45

En Plein-Air	46
Of Poets and Purveyors	47
The Pruning	48
Where I Dwell	49
Winter's Renaissance	50

The Aerodynamics of the Muse

Wilbur and Orville, fanciers of flight,
used paper airplanes to dream up invention.
Poems, like paper airplanes, are prototypes
of the real thing, whose unfolding is in the weight
of the paper, and how that paper is folded edge upon edge.
Launch is tantamount to lift, but it's the will of the wind
that gentles an ultralight to circle back like a boomerang
and land in the hand, shears a winged objet d'art
to crash down and say *start over,* lifts a complicated craft
with clipped wings to soar over the city, arc into a loop
de loop, sail through a candle's flame, and land,
unscathed, at your feet.

The Secrets of Trees

Three birch trees stand in a cluster, lend contrast to the forest,
cast catkins to the playful vole, the red squirrel.
Three birch trees rooted together, black on white bark
easily stripped, bent and sewn into service.

One tree is courted by a woodpecker, pileated, powerful,
he whittles and riddles her slender trunk with holes
that drain her sap wells but draw sips from tiny acrobats
that hum, hover and flash jewels to bless her.

The middle tree lacked sunlight, grew slowly as others soared.
Afforded a view like no other, her barren, leafless canopy
extends jazz hands to the spirited sky, sun and gypsy clouds—
wonders that outweigh the shadow-talk of cutting her down.

The third tree's flesh is pulled in opposite directions by three
metal feeders laden with seed that swing from brackets nailed
to her trunk, but elicit trills of orioles and chipping sparrows,
and the thrill of a thousand feet and feathers.

Three birch trees stand rooted in amity, share unspoken secrets.
Rest comes when darkness drives away suitors, limbs entwined
like sleeping sisters that rouse at the other's sudden shiver.
They lean in, hold each other up, *sorelle per sempre*.

Songbird-Raptor

The farmhouse chair chirped on wooden planks
as she lifted her cup from its saucer, lowered her head
to the crimson contents of elderberry tea.

Outside, a shrike, songbird-raptor, black, white
and grey plumage so handsome on the hedgerow,
scans for prey over the pasture, hooked beak in tandem
with head turn, ebony eyes but a glint on a dark mask.

Beseeched by the whir of the bee, the wren, the sparrow,
his white wings flash over meadow milkweed, then blur
in a hover-hunt, to impale his prize on a thorn.

Drifters

I recall savory bites into hand-cut ham sandwiches,
wax paper wrapped wonder bread somewhat soggy
with relish and mustard at picnic tables in truck stops,
the whir of eighteen-wheelers headed east, or west,
one filled with all we owned.

I recall turns next to Dad in the front seat of the rambler,
Mom and siblings asleep in the back.
I nodded in and out of blue and white Midwestern dreams
where sails separate sky from water, dart around buoys
like schools of fish, the keel's thrill-song,
the sail's bow to gusty winds, the hull's heavenward heave,
toes tucked tightly in hiking straps as we lean backwards
into air over racing water, our faith in the counterbalance,
the ride back down, the turn of the tiller,
the swing of the boom, the spill of the wind,
the rush starboard—to yet another port.

The Last Time

Rain freezes on the windowpane,
blurs trees that twist from concrete cracks,
their branches splayed against brick buildings
as if under arrest.
This, the longest I've lived anywhere.
I reach into the bread bag, two dried heels,
grab a pen to find it inkless, a pencil, no eraser,
it's time for me to go

to my job up littered stairwells in smoky flats
where guarded men or anxious women live alone
hunched over ashtrays as they cup caffeine,
attend to voices only they can hear.
I coax them to open curtains, raise a window,
fill a hummingbird feeder, then we wait and wait
for an iridescent angel that never comes,
it's time to for me go

down a road that winds and winds up in a cove
with a heron, a blue one, belly deep in shallows
under a willow's sweep that shelters my tired talisman
gone grey from following me town to town,
his mournful coo a call for back up:
a wisdom of owls who'll raise their eyes,
a bullfrog to bellow *bullshit,* a scold of jays to jeer me
if ever, from a pier up here I should say
it's time for me to go.

My Grown Daughter Asks About Her Grandma

Anxious to share my news, I hurried through the airport,
hand on my abdomen, new life inside that was you
—only six months to go.

Anxious to share her news, grandma, wet eyes, long embrace,
hand on her abdomen, a mass inside, pancreatic cancer
—only six months to go.

Funeral Flowers

It was three below zero when she returned from the funeral
to a Fed-Ex bouquet box left on the deck.

Deep red roses with stiff outer petals encircled by calla lilies
rimmed in ice crystals, like fluted margaritas.

She trimmed the frozen stems, peeled the outmost petals,
cropped the lily tops, put aspirin in their water.

Next morning the flowers' exterior edges had darkened,
so, the same surgery and nutrients, then the next day, and the next.

That sundown she gathered the whittled, withered buds in her arms
and let go, when even hope cried out—*enough.*

Bowls of July

I sat down with a bowl of April
strawberries, store-bought,
red on bottom, white on top,
ripe enough.

My grandson, the picky one
stretched out his hand.
I searched for the best.
He bit, winced and spit.

Forget April bowls, little one.
Wait, cultivate
juice down your chin
big old grin bowls of July.

The Breakup

Mama, he's a new soul, a clean slate,
first string plucked on a new tune,
lid flung open on a box of confectionary,
each grab a sugar rush.

But mama, I'm an old soul, a fossil,
a phantom, a cicada's drum song,
each cycle more in tune
to the hum of memory's marrow,
the lull of lesson-grizzled bones.

To Her Daughter, at the Onset

Do you remember the night the hall light burned out,
the scrape of your outstretched palms against cold,
bumpy walls as you searched and stumbled,
your blanket a safety net to our bedroom?
It was as always, yet unfamiliar.

Do you remember the goldfish when we returned
from Yellowstone, Sop n' Wet's slow swim
through murky water around furry fish toys,
different from their darting dance in clear, clean water?
It was as always, yet unfamiliar.

Do you see the topography of your hand, its candy-cane scar,
lotus tattoo, half-moon nailbeds, calloused palms?
These, the blueprints of your life will be the map to my heart
as it remembers to beat, but forgets the slip of your hand,
the sound of your name, beloved as always—yet unfamiliar.

Tributaries of a Dream

A deep purple candle burns unconstrained
on cardboard in the center of Dad's table.

Wax spills in all directions like the dead end channels
and long, lazy stretches of Missouri's Table Rock Lake

—remember how it coaxed our craft onward as if pulled
by a string, until lost in the Ozark's hunched embrace?

As the candle lays out tributaries
my 94-year-old Dad shuffles around it, scrapes

and peels up wax, drops it back into its base.
He looks up, poses a riddle, or instructs—I can't remember,

but when I awake, his message, metamorphic in its impression,
leaves me tearful as it drifts out of reach.

Was it to burn concentrated, contained, slow and steady,
or pour out uncharted, like water finding its level,

in paths more dilute, some running on, others stopping
at dead ends to be scraped up, reused?

And, as my watchful father scurried to recycle the spent wax,
was he tending to his candle, or mine?

The Last of the Lightbulbs

(For Anita, 1931-2017)

Anita's husband kept lightbulbs in the basement,
doled them out as needed, ceded the key, she mused,
moments before he died, when an unusual number of lights
burned out, sending her up and down the stairs.

Years later in a crowded church hall comes the sequel.
I'm the one who walks by when she falters, grabs my arm,
gasps for oxygen from a tank that can't keep up.
At the table she chides me with *stranger*, but as we catch up
she softens to *baby*, elicits my middle-aged smile.

Anita retells the lightbulb story, bright mouth
that housed a brassy tongue, now blueish.
Uneasy, I shush her, *you'll be ok*, but her expression reveals
she's been hushed before, and this may be her last telling.

I realize she led me to her table, this moment, her witness.
I look down, search for words, come up short.
She leans in, takes my hand, whispers breathlessly,
This week, an unusual number of lightbulbs burned out.
I hold her stare, squeeze her hand, and nod.

In Autumn We Purchase Northwoods Lakefront Property

We upset a mud puddle's perfect cloud reflection as we drive
down the dirt lane of the gated community, dead quiet,
and come to rest near the end of the road, our plot covered
in leaves, above the lake's mirrored still life of tamaracks and pine.

An unkindness of ravens descends to broadcast
this is *their* place with sounds like lawnmowers, car engines
—imitators in a shadowland of plantations.
Intending to be stiff competition, we hold our ground.

The stony silence of this elder community hangs
gossamer like lake mist as we explore tight labyrinth lanes,
quell mortal thoughts, shudder and depart downhill
through the gates of The Lakeside Garden of Sleep.

The Sun's Position

I walked a winter road weighed down
not by heavy garments but by the horrid breath
of hate in the news, editorials, words of a neighbor.

I lumbered such a distance I had to rally to outrace
the dark hours that now outnumbered light,
my earthly impact so slight I could hardly lift my legs.

A melted rivet of water chiseled a hollow in the snowscape.
There, a bit of thaw to arouse the vernal season and remind
that in time, the sun will always break the back of winter.

After the Shootings, a Congregation

No solace found in the sermon
we turned to look at one another.
Across the aisle a bald baby
on the shoulder of his mother
spotted another in the pew behind.

They tremored toward each other,
chubby arms extended,
hyper-articulating
until each mom
leaned in.
They increased their pitch,
eyes met,
lips touched.
They embraced.

I stood a silent witness
to a place from which
we could
begin again.

Opportunity

Jose's parents bend, cut, toss cabbages,
rummaged clothes a shield in unflinching sun.
They cup Jose's cherubic face, review their rules,
tighten their embrace before the long ride to find work,
limp, as the pulsing lights of la migra reflect off the gas pump.

Eight-year-old Jose obeys, stays in the flat
until his neighbor, now legal, drives him to school,
where curiosity's tinder is ignited with Lewis and Clark,
volcanoes of vinegar, field trips to Black Creek Library,
practice seats at the Timber Rattlers.

Jose, unattended after school, large book in a little lap,
pries open mathematical problems like sweet tangerines,
grasps the scientific, pours over the worldly, believes.
No cell phone, no x-box, no video games,
but an eager heir alone, in a land of opportunity.

Fifth Floor Children's Hospital, Providence, RI

After needle pokes, X-rays, contrast coursing
through tender veins to the clunk of an MRI,
after the day's drip of poisons into youthful bodies,
of parent's supplication, hopes severed, comes darkness.

The children are led, the very ill wheeled, teens wade
in dark to gather at windows, flashlights in hand.
Squeals of delight blanket little ones as residents shine
kaleidoscopes of color at them
—flashlights, porchlights, headlights, spotlights,
squad cars, firetrucks, sky scrapers, tugboats and churches
blink good-night, and the fledglings shine their own good-night
lights to the well-wishers below, invisible strangers.
At eight-thirty nightly, darkness, life and breath are transcended
here in the midst of Providence.

Little Girl Dancing in a Short Museum Film

Her miniature knee-length coat
has whimsical big buttons that bob
reflections of the sun and sky
with each twirl off her mother's hand,
the hand not clasped to her infant brother.

This little veteran of short films,
family photographs, boundless affection,
dances, the camera's zoom a familiar playmate,
dances, among throngs she does not notice
are not noticing, not even her mother,
dances, closest to the entrance
they are pushed up against.

This tiny progeny of her parent's sweat
and aspiration, of their thirst and expectation
dances tethered, dances spritely until the film's
final moment freezes the big buttons on her
miniature knee-length coat as they mirror
the sun, sky, and swastikas of the men
behind the camera.

Plough Horses and Carriages

Dale, a retired Amish plough horse
newly renamed by the carriage company
side steps puddles, walks around sewers,
resists right turns, defies stop signs.
He plods past Charleston-green doors
and shutters of Civil War dwellings,
Federal, Georgian, Gothic, Queen Anne.
Dale's eyes fix upon haint blue historic
homes of the Gullah, decedents of slaves,
ghosts on every veranda, lulled
by the cobblestone clatter of a plough horse,
driven by habit, harnessed to history.

The carriage driver's slap of the switch
directs Dale through ornate cemeteries honored still
a century later, past unnoted, unnamed graves of slaves
below southern live oaks whose twisted, trunk-sized limbs
forced groundward by wind, drought, fire and sea spray
persist skyward, sweet with acorns and evergreen leaves.
Dale nuzzles the newest sprout's tap roots that feed
on the fecund longing entombed below, lulled
by the cobblestone clatter of a plough horse,
driven by habit, harnessed to history.

Le Jardin de Claude Monet

Tour guides in varied languages lead masses
around his pond while visitors obscure
horizon and bank to volley for vantage spots.

Their bright umbrellas stem from pastel coats
like blossoms all over his garden path, an image
of *Water Lilies* through the blur of droplets on my glasses.

In its pivot away from advancing swarms
my camera finds its focus on a French gardener,
whose unamused eyes size up yet another invader.

His slow nod directs my gaze to a vacant section
of reflective pond ablaze with red rhododendrons,
yellow-eyed forget-me-nots, iridescent iris and narcissi.

Hues shift with the roll and lift of rain clouds,
the sun emerges, the colors pop,
my camera clicks, the gardener smiles.

The Return to the Ice Caves

For the first time in five years bone-chilling temperatures
return to form an ice bridge to caves of the south shore.
In ten days ten thousand come from as far as Japan to trek
this treacherous mile on a lake the Ojibwa named The Great Sea.

Bits of blood on unseen ice heaves call for cleats and ski poles.
Explorers, silenced by waterfalls solidified in their spill from cliffs
of striated sandstone creviced with needles, tucked and twinkling,
labor towards cave mouths that bare enormous icicle teeth,
and tongues of scalloped silver under sapphire skies.

So spiritual, these sanctuaries that appear frozen in time
but change day to day, drop by drop—nature's testimony
to the power of time and tenacity.

Incoming

Snowmelt falls from horizontals,
soggy roofs, barren branches,
plump propane tanks.
Like sugar cookie dough
dropped from a spoon,
piles of snow remain
on the slats of the lake porch.
In the periphery, the sweep of a storm.

Snow glazed shores stretched tight
like a white suede drum crack
as lightning begins its percussive attack.
Rain torrents paint ice fragments angry-black,
icicle islands, like bumper cars in an arcade,
collide, burst, and bow to the incoming season.

How the Universe Guides Us

My seasonal neighbor, Mary, shared her adult son had liver cancer.
I had no chocolate chips, oats, bananas, blueberries, or raisins.
Far from a store, old-fashioned molasses cookies, the only choice.

I winced at blackstrap molasses bought in error, stronger, less
sweet, double rolled the dark dough balls in sugar to compensate,
plated them on pale green paper finished with lavender ribbons.

It began to rain so we drove rather than walk the steep forest path
to the cottage where their pickup was idling, packed for winter.
We exchanged goodbyes after sharing his dismal diagnosis.

I handed them the plate, bemoaned our bare pantry's only offering
of blackstrap cookies, explained they were coated with extra sugar.
Mary looked at her husband, teared up, waved from their truck.

In spring they joined our campfire to tell of their son's memorial,
how his favorite cookie was molasses, blackstrap, twice rolled
in sugar, how they took comfort in a few, sent the rest to him.

My Morning Buzz

I take my seat on the lakeside deck in the treetops
as cicadas motor a kayak's slip behind birch and pine.
A mini fighter jet roars in tight to my robe of roses,
me, sheepish, as his sugar water has gone dry.

Yellow finches launch dive bombs and fly-bys
toward their feeder, my chair a rock on their runway.
A woodpecker whacks cartoonish on scanty suet,
rearing his red head with each hole hammered.

I dodge a finch, stare down a hummingbird, wave a white
Kleenex, whistle Chickadee as I do not speak Finch.
Channeling this ambassador's two-note tempo of *feed me-me*
we settle into symbiosis, birds awaiting food, and me, my coffee.

Toads on the Lake Road

No moon to light the twisty road,
the rain-soaked woods, the night bestowed.
Leaves oddly litter the vernal lane,
fog rises, slumps on its mirrored plane.
We peer between drops and wiper blades,
are those fallen leaves that jerk and sway?
They pile up like popcorn popping,
frenzied droves from the forest, hopping.

We travel serpentine, driver and spotter,
necks pinned to windshield in view of the fodder,
shrieking the squish, lamenting the slaughter,
cheering the dodge as they leap from pooled water.
We trip as we race down our walkway all drenched,
open porch windows, clear off the bench,
collapse as this cohort of scholars, savants
of winter's harsh tenure, these lovesick gallants
descend the hill to swampy expanse
all agog—in peep and circumstance.

Let Ornithology Call the Day

A phoebe awakens me on Monday.
Phoebe. *Phoebe?* Phoebe. *Phoebe?*
I'll stop questioning everything.

An eastern towhee on Tuesday.
Drink your tea, drink your tea.
I'll sip jasmine on the sun porch.

A robin on Wednesday.
Cheer-up cheerily, cheer-up cheerily.
I'll release yesterday's funk.

A hermit thrush on Thursday.
Here I am right near you.
I'll sort the photos in the shoebox.

A crow calls on Friday.
Caw, caw, caw.
I'll call back my friends.

The ovenbird on Saturday.
Teacher-teacher-teacher-teacher.
I'll read Rumi today.

On Sunday, a mourning dove coos
soft as my lover's sigh.
I'll lay lilacs on his grave.

The Reset

As we hurried down the hall you shared you were broken,
eyes full as a math book crammed with proofs confirmed
or rebutted in the balance of your amply open mind,
each arm of the scale heaped with theories to tip it

this way or that, your course adjusted accordingly.
Bleary and full, the exhausted eyes of a seeker,
a giver, delicate and strong like a sun-sparked web,
you throw threads into the wilderness to bridge

gaps one thinks they cannot cross.
I could not find words in the hall that day,
but today a spider lit on the forestay of my sail,
its silk aglow in sunlight as it spanned

the unthinkable distance from island to boat.
Did you know when part of a web becomes broken
the rest of the silk stretches beyond capacity
to reset itself, stronger than ever?

Flashbacks of a Retiree: Call Me Ginny

Hearing a pundit dismiss gender disparities
I saw my youthful arm reach for my first degree,
excited to be one of two women admitted to my graduate
school of choice. But there was this professor.

It began when he asked for input at a weekly research roundtable.
Why wouldn't gibbons, an arboreal species,
favor his novel feeder placed high in the cage?
Why do they still eat from the lower dish?

You're using both fruit and vegetables, I offered,
they're going to the feeder that has fruit left,
like a kid that leaves peas on a plate
but grabs a treat. The smile left his face.

When I applied for a graduate assistant job
he said, you have little ones at home.
I longed to say so do you,
So do you.

When I turned in an analytical paper
he questioned if I authored it, then
to a series of groans required copies
of journal articles quoted from then on.

Under his watchful eye as he paced the room
he directed us to write a paper in class.
I tore into the task as if to save the lives
of my little family, dependent on me.

When my graduate research won first place
at the science fair he said I schmoozed the judges.
The time I was first to solve one of his verbal puzzles
he said, you must have heard this one before.

The "A's" I worked hard for could not be obtained in his classes.
He returned my thesis draft red-inked with reworded phrases.
When revised as directed, he scrawled out his own phrases
thinking they were mine, and reworded them again. And again.

Did I mention he sometimes called me and the only other woman
by the wrong names, framed as *Miss, ah, Sandy; Miss, ah, Barb?*
Often aghast we endured to get our degrees, all the while waiting
to hear him call out *Miss, ah, Ginny.*

Endangered

Nature has made up her mind that what cannot defend itself shall not be defended
—Ralph Waldo Emerson

Ferocity has her,
empty-handed swordfighter,
in a choke hold.
Her blocking techniques—
the sweeping low block,
the rising palm block,
the hands together block
belie the percussive racing rhythm
of her unarmed heart.

For years she's bypassed battle
and for years she has been battered
as she masters this conceivably deadly dance,
its grace, solidarity and strength, in self-defense.
Pushed to the precipice she will circle you
with a flurry of flying jump kicks, knee strikes,
a scissors strike close to the spleen, a stomp
just short of your heart.
Spared and supine, she'll cover *you* with a coat
of humility as you slither away.

Sated, safe, she'll take leave in stillness
to breathe, breathe, breathe back in
what was lost, seek caritas, then steel herself
for the inevitable next round with Kipling's tale
of the mongoose, who in defense of family and self
dodges and dances just outside the cobra's deadly strike,
seemingly afraid, but secretly skilled.
Unbeknownst to the cobra, the mongoose
is resistant to its venom, capable of a kill-shot.

For years she's bypassed battle
and for years she has been battered,
slashes here, wounds there, have rendered her immune.
You see her olive branch as a failing, her, a frail-ing,
but know this: in this conceivably deadly dance,
she is the mongoose.

A Heart Swells

(For Pat)

First her mother after two surgeries,
her brother by his own hand,
another by alcohol, her closest sister,
double hit lymphoma, her father combative
on the memory care ward two thousand miles away.
She visits her husband's father in a small room
on Primrose Lane, dementia causing him
to inquire over and over how is her family?

She couldn't attend his funeral from the ICU,
they thought it was flu until she coded.
They intubated and revived her, said stress
sent a surge of adrenaline that stunned her heart,
caused her left ventricle to balloon into the shape
of a Japanese octopus trap, a *takotsubo*.

She resides in a wing near Primrose Lane,
husband close by, they work towards recovery.
Doctors call it takotsubo cardiomyopathy.
We who struggle to find words and ways to help
call it a broken heart.

The Last Flicker

It was then she made her decision,
the day the flicker flew into the window,

its slam so severe she dropped a dish.
She knew him well, the curve of his bill,

regal red patch on the nape of his neck,
the flare of his tail. But how could she have known

his belly's perfect pattern of black and white,
or that his under-wings were gilded?

She watched his mate swoop over him,
light on a limb above, begged her husband

to wait a bit, should the flicker revive.
But he pummeled past her, declared it dead,

heaved a shovel beneath, flung it into the woods.
It was then she made her decision.

En Plein-Air

Led by the wooded curve of a crushed granite drive,
I park for the ekphrastic event in the last spot,
driver's door close to an old, tall tree.
I slide out, face tight to a red pine's primal canvas.

Scattered in clay colored ridges are onyx scales
like slaty cleavage, crusty furrows that look as though
they could be lifted, built up, split apart, reassembled.
A Cézanne. A Picasso. A Juan Gris.

As daylight shifts, embers ascend from the bark's
darkest carrels, lucent pigments flare like doves flung
into opaline flight above schools of coral-colored salmon,
fluoresced in seas of earthen umber.

Frozen in this humble drive beside the ancient tree
I watch Monet's brush, his choppy strokes, his liaison
with form and light—the poet's, the painter's desiderata.

Of Poets and Purveyors

Thunderheads unfold, heads in their hands.
Dandelions, milkweed, clover
are dismissed as weeds, their purveyor,
the rusty patched bumblebee, endangered,
the meadow, a flag without its breeze.

Who decides what's a flower, what's a weed?

Dandelions, milkweed, clover
track the sun, plant roots deep,
defy drought, backs all but broken
—with seed.

The Pruning

Her houseplant, a fig tree, grows lopsided, spindly,
pale limbs lethargic over its gifted Grecian urn.
Pruning, she moves to the window side where it
it flourishes, deep green, ambiently nourished.

Stripped of the unruly, the streamlined branches
bleed thick and milky, then seal themselves
from what is lost to send shoots in all directions.
A cutting is left levitating in mid-air.

The overcluttered fig tree, stressed for space,
sent out a tendril to traverse the expanse between
inside screen and outside glass, filled it with fine
fig greenery, its sentinel shoot now suspended.

She pots the shoot, silences her cell, closes her laptop,
slips out the screen door, climbs in her kayak,
wind-mills away from worldly into the world,
lighter, pared, buoyant, bared, levitating in mid-air.

Where I Dwell

I dwell in Possibility—
A fairer House than Prose—
   Emily Dickenson

The heirloom tomatoes that wound around
the treetop balcony rail
away from pests winged and hoofed
were religiously fertilized,
grew globular, green, and meaty—
but not until October.

And so the vines, short on sun,
drained of form, drained of color—
grew wary of Frost.
Experts enjoined me to toss them,
grow cabbage, grow carrots—
there are no tomatoes in these woods.

Too many for my narrow hands,
I gather into my work apron
each unseasoned satin orb,
place some in a bag to ripen,
and for the rest—Possibility—
green tomato curry, green tomato cake,
fried green tomatoes.

Winter's Renaissance

I peer out the window at tiny tracks of a woodland vole
that graze the grey-blue snow shaded by the roof's soffit.
A different life, the woodland vole, from a meadow vole
whose neck cranes upward in fear of talons.

His comfort's in the woods, a fragrant bower of balsams,
rich with roots, stems and seeds, burrowed into crispy brown
oak leaves, tucked in a coverlet of snow, swaddled by trees.

I nestle into my chair, light the almost spent candle
beside books abandoned in the hectic seasons,
tighten a wrap, scan the woodland windows
mindful that winter proffers more than respite.

Black smoke spirals up from the sconce in a last gasp,
vanishes into the ceiling, wax consumed, brass already cold,
leaving a scent-burst of birthday candles, a life flash of memories.
The clock chimes; I pick up my pen.

About the Author

Nancy Austin has lived on both coasts and numerous places between, leading to an eclectic life and outlook. In pursuit of what the universe has laid in her path, it sometimes seems as though there's a string attached to her forehead, and she writes in between its tugs. She has settled in the Northwoods of Wisconsin, relishes an occasional adventure and enjoys visits from family and friends.

Nancy strives for accessible poetry, easily digested with an aftertaste of some sort. As she weaves together her stories with the stories of others, she hopes to connect to those who share similar threads, and especially to those who don't.

She has been published in various journals including *Adanna, Ariel, Bramble, Gyroscope Review, Midwestern Gothic, Sheepshead Review, Verse Wisconsin, Wisconsin Poets Calendars,* and *Zingara*. Her first collection of poems is titled *Remnants of Warmth* (2016, Aldrich Press), available on Amazon or through Kelsay Books.

www.ingramcontent.com/pod-product-compliance
Lightning Source LLC
LaVergne TN
LVHW040040090426
835510LV00037B/586